Alchemy of the Soul II: Sublimation
ISBN: 9789090350400

*To Mom and Dad,
specially now, that I'm healing from so many
things.*

*To all the people in my life that, in one way
or another, made me grow.*

*To Gheorghe, you inspire me every day and
you know this wouldn't have seen the light if
it wasn't for you.*

*And to all the people that keep trying doesn't
matter what, that are working so hard and
doing their best to overcome, to be better and
to live more fully*

I was so caught up in
my own warm emotions
when he put his arms around me
that I couldn't read his.

I should've been paying attention
maybe I wouldn't be so lost now.

I support, no, I back you up;
I'll stand by your side and help you fight,
the same that you still do for me.

I'll keep putting up my smile for you,
I'll keep cracking jokes and playing fool
if that way I can bring a smile to your face.

Even if I'm unsure and broken after all this,
you haven't stopped being my friend;

You've shown me respect, pride, and instilled an unusual
inspiration and illusion in me.
You're brilliant, so much light in you even in these times
when your shadows are equally strong.

You're fascinating to me, in your lonely ways,
and I can see now that you love in other shapes,

unbeknown to me,
but that could teach me a valuable lesson,
a lesson of patience and calmness.

Even if inside I'm still craving your arms
and your warmth; this will suffice.

This will be enough.
And I will be happy to spend the time I can as a friend to
you.

I'm not renouncing to who I am,
I'm not renouncing to my intensity
I'm just learning to relax a little bit.

This is new, and exciting to me.
I'm ready

I doubt myself so hard many times
I doubt this we have.

But somehow in the midst of my worst,
lowest moments, I can't shake
the feeling that my heart is in the right place.

I've said this with others
only to be completely wrong in the end.
But somehow I keep hearing
that small voice saying
"Don't give up, don't give up on him"

Maybe I just don't want to accept the truth,
maybe I can't move on, but this feeling
tells me that my heart is in the right place.

"We create what we believe in," you said to me once
and I do believe in you
so so much.

From Alchemy of the Soul I

Sublimation: *noun. From the Latin word sublimare, meaning "to rise to a higher status." The transition of a solid straight on to gaseous state, caused by the exposure to external pressure.*
Known as a type of distillation, it is the boiling and condensation of the previously pressured solution to increase its purity, an important process within the magnum opus.

This agitation of the spirit is necessary to ensure that no impurities from the lower personality are incorporated into the next and final process. "It rises from Earth to Heaven and descends again to Earth" is how the twelve keys of the Emerald tablet describe it, which implies that it combines within Itself the powers of both the Above and the Below.

By this process, the spiritualization of the body is possible, as well as the spirit made corporeal through working with the heavenly attributes of the philosophical Mercury, the First Matter of the Three Essences; representing the second or higher state of the Water Element.

Psychologically, it consists of a variety of introspective techniques that analyse and channel the subconscious impulses of the lower psyche by integrating them, an operation of casting light to the Shadow self by work and fire, rising the contents of the psyche to the highest level, the purification of the Self, all that we truly are and can be.

It is a Circulation of the energy, as the Mercury-Hermes messenger of the Gods, traveling from the Underworld of the copying mechanisms and hidden valuable gems to the higher realms of Sun-Apollo realization, where these treasures can become a useful solidified light, full of transformative power for the personal development.

It is the ultimate realization of the power of higher love as an extension of divine nature, a tool to fight against hate and act as unifier of the collective into the deep waters of the primordial sea, the original source of all life.

DESTINY

*Not necessarily everything that happens has
a hidden meaning, but everything that
happens does for a reason that suit your
choices*

I keep making space
in my life for people
that won't make up
space for me in theirs.

I don't want to be too clingy, but still

I feel like the dog who waits under the table,
just in case some crumbs fall to the ground.

Begging for scraps of affection.

I'm torn between believing or not,
if I believe, I'll be hurt again,
probably.

But if I don't then what's left?

This could be a shit, this could be the end;
I could die now, and that's it,

And I'm telling myself *'Which side
do you want to see?'*

The negative is there, the rejection,
and I don't want to avoid it,
that would be really unwise.

But I don't want to focus on it, either;
And I'm making a godly effort
to stay on the positive side.

'Which side am I choosing?'

And every time I choose the positive one
I tell myself

'You're such a fool and you're going to get hurt so much'

I don't choose just anyone,
and choosing someone is a rational matter.

That's why, when I choose,
when I allow myself to fall for someone,
when I deem them worthy of my time,
I give everything.
I give my all, and I expect nothing back

And it's so messed up, so killing,
when you give yourself away completely and
you get pushed out.

I don't allow many people here, inside,
and when I do, they stay there for a long time.
Even if I'm rejected, my all stays with them.

And I started thinking,
if I keep giving myself out,
what's going to be left of me?

But I can't stop it.
This is how I am, this is *who* I am
and honestly, I don't want to change it.

This fragility might kill me,
one day.

But I think I shouldn't change it.

I'm doing a massive effort
to stop waiting for you

I would wait my whole life,
even if everybody
is telling me I shouldn't;
I would totally do it.

This is something I must learn,
I must do it on my own.

I can't keep waiting for someone that doesn't want to
make the slightest effort.

Even if I want to, I can't

Even if I'd like to, I shouldn't.

Friendship means that I'll remember you
in the smallest of things.

Friendship means that I'll send you
Instagram stories, or tag you
on random facebook posts I think you'll like.

Friendship means that out of the blue I'll write you a
message, something unimportant,
something silly,
trivial.

Friendship doesn't mean that I'll be waiting
or the time that you want to be around to come.

You know, just because we're "just friends"
doesn't mean that we don't give and receive,
trust and respect.
Reciprocation.

I can't be doing all the effort to be
by your side if all you're doing is
kicking me out of your life.

I would have stayed, but there's a limit
to the amounts of kicks someone can tolerate.

…..

(*You're lying to yourself*)

I know I'm lying to myself but,
sometimes you have to convince yourself

That enough is enough,
that you did all you could,
that you should not give more.

That there's a limit,
that you can't be subject to the whims of those who

Won't reciprocate.

I don't want gratitude, or servitude, or to be given back the
same I give

But what I totally don't expect is to be paid off with
a kick in the chest.

Over and over again.

Don't
Don't look at me
Don't

Don't look at me as if you still wanted me
to be a part of your life.
Don't look at me as if you don't understand.

You made this choice,
and you made it for both.
You didn't allow my opinion on it.
So don't look at me.

Don't
Don't look at me as if you wanted me nearby
when that's a lie.

It's a lie It's a lie It's a lie It's a lie It's a lie
It's a lie

IT'S A LIE

YOU LIED AND I BELIEVED

SUCH A FOOL!

I'm just a cynic who
wants so desperately to have hope that
tricks herself into believing.
Anything and anyone

Anything and anyone.

I'll turn you unto poems,
into words, emotions pouring on paper,
as trying to let go so hard is
not getting me anywhere.

I'll turn you into ink,
made of the tears I cried (un)necessarily.

I'll turn you into lines and turns,
resembling all the movement you made over my skin.

Since it seems you won't disappear,
I'll transform you,
put you to my South
and turn my eyes to the path on the front,
to the Northern lights
and the Stars that guide me now.

It's the weekend and I'm dressing up
on golden sparks of light for my special man

(*He's not coming*)

So charming and funny, with the godly smile

(*He's not coming*)

And we're going to hang out and be
the envy of everyone

(*He's not coming*)

Hours pass like they're minutes or less,
ticking out chores meanwhile you sleep.

(*He's not coming*)

And I keep holding on for your call,
but it's OK; you're tired and I don't mind

(*He's not coming*)
He's not coming
He's not coming
He's not coming

The mirror fell and shattered, in every wisp
the reflection of the child.
You were just like him.

Am I not enough?

Am I not worth it?

Do I know already you won't come,
did I know he wouldn't come?

Or was I just crushing my own hope?

Am I? Now?

Why wouldn't you come?
Why wouldn't you love me?
What have I done wrong?

'Nothing' I tell the child,
'You did nothing wrong'

CYCLE

*It's all about running improving tests
and keeping trying until eventually it works
out*

I met with you out of spite,
to be honest.
Doesn't mean I didn't like you in the first place.

I wanted to feel desired once more,
not cold like a leftover.

Funny, because you were so worried that
you might not be able to please me
that you didn't realise that, at that precise moment,
you gave me what I was truly looking for,
that which even I didn't know I was searching.

And you held me in your arms, and cherished me
so much that I knew.

This was no one-time stand.
It was bright, as the skies at night,
and I was howling inside,
like werewolves howl for their prey.

I'm afraid
what if I'm wrong again?

I'm afraid
that I'm misjudging a character again

I'm afraid
that I want to make an all-in move again
I'm afraid

To trust
and fall
again.

I'm walking on lead feet
but still, I'm afraid

I saw a book named 'be afraid and do it anyway'

The moon, hiding in the south with the archer,
and the warrior just standing
with the beginning of the path lying at his feet,
untouched.

Now I stand my ground but *'where do I stand?'*

There are a million things I want to do, and a million
things I need to let go of for that.

Like the warrior, afraid of the journey but undertaking it
anyway,
wondering
'where is this road going to take me?'
While the moon hides in the South with the Archer.

And you don't know, you never know;
but you start walking anyway because,
what good can come out of staying still anyway?

The worst part of it all is
the ever-present question:

How long will it last?

Am I making actual progress or....

Is this just a manic episode before
depression hits back and I fall on my knees....

once more?

Like the eye of the hurricane,
or the quietness before the storm.

Like the spring rainy day after an entire week of sun.

I can't even enjoy it while I'm ok

I catch myself sometimes
running my fingers through the scar,

Pushing and prodding and never letting it heal

And in a burst of fury,
a moment of epiphany I decided, yes,

I've decided to tear apart my hull,

To expose my flesh and bones all raw;

Like that it would be even again, no scar,
no wound at all.

Just a clean, soft, polished surface,
ready to grow green and fresh again.

Like a flower in full bloom, moist with tears of joy

I held a rock in my hands,
maybe strange in shape but,
I found it beautiful nevertheless.

I held a rock in my hands,
even if some people didn't understand,
but there was a reason why,
I chose it, and I picked it up and brought it home.

And I put it on a cabinet, taking it out
from time to time, but forgetting at others
that it was there for me.

I tumbled it, and tossed it in the air, maybe
unintentionally too rough.

And I just thought '*It's a rock,
so solid, will never break....*

...Like I do'

But one day I was too careless, indeed,
and the stone fell and

I made a crack on it.

I looked at it from above,
telling myself it was not damaged,
but when I picked it up, it was undeniable

I broke it.

And from inside the two halves I saw then
a beautiful quartz, hidden

Strong yet precious,
something to cherish and protect.

And I promised myself,
to tenderly care,
and never treat you wrong, my dear stone.

A valley, beautiful;
whatever you might think or say.
A regal peak, pointy and slim,
a solemn coomb, immutable one might think,
but that shakes and trembles
with the laughter of a kid;

Strong lines framing it all,
and twin pools,
severe and cutting that
turn to green fields in the daylight
and to silvery moon in the rain.

The peace I find
in this serene beauty,
can't be described.

Maybe it's soon to say but,
I'm realising, slowly,
that you have the flowers that make
my butterflies flutter
in contentment

I want to sing for you.

Do you understand,
do you?

Do you really understand?

You make me want to sing for you.

I'll have to thank you after all;

Thank you for shattering me,
when I glued myself back, I did it better.
Stronger.

Fixed few things on the way.

Honestly, now,
I only feel sorry for you.

You, who go through life without living,
with the skin intact,
just out of fear
of bonding,
of loving
and losing.

I feel sorry for you but,
I can't heal you.

You must do that yourself.
I just hope you realize before it's too late.

Cursing and
crushing
my own hope
(*he's not going to call*)
out of fear of attachment
(*too late, too late*)
my triggers screaming
(*abandon! abandon!*
who would make you a priority?
you're not worth! you're not worth!)
Senseless, as you've proven the contrary
with acts and words.

I'm impaled
by a sword through the chest;
a sword I'm holding myself
on my left hand.
And the handle is burning my skin.

Such a contradiction,
too needy and too proud,
and egoistical enough to state my duties
but not acknowledge yours.

Terrible

A part of me wishes you well
(away from me, though)
another part just doesn't care
and says it's not my business anymore.

The problem is that some other part,
quite big,
just wishes to see you suffer
eternally
for what you did.
Without possibility of redemption.

And that's no good,
it means you still have something left behind.
Here.

I thought it was overcomed
(and mostly it is)
But it would be easier if I didn't have to see you.

Could you please stop looking at me?
This choice, you took for the both of us,
you have no right to lay eyes on me anymore.

If
I'm due to heal,
to let go and not hold
onto it
anymore
I understand that I'll have to forgive
all of this you did to me
without receiving an apology for it,
as you won't offer it
and probably in your eyes you did
nothing wrong.

I'm not one to judge
if you did wrong or right.
I'll just say that
everything we do
have an impact on people
and on their emotions.

Still, I'll have to forgive
if I want to kick you out of here

SPIRAL

*And you keep climbing up and up, and
suddenly you're able to see things with
perspective and you just wish that you don't
fall back again, and that you could reach
down a hand to those under*

I've been quite good for a while,
and "quite good" doesn't mean
that I don't struggle,
some days more than others;
but, comparatively, I've been
quite good for a while.

Maybe that's the reason why,
I don't remember

Was I that miserable in my worst?

I don't remember.

One day you'll regret the things you didn't do
just because you were afraid of the outcome.
Just because the "what if's"

I don't think I was like that,
even in my worst.

But then again,
I throw myself headfirst at everything,
that's why I always end up broken
in a thousand pieces

And from all my cracks and crevices,
a golden light will emerge,
like the Sun at the entrance of a Cave,
after wandering in its deep, dark recesses.

And this will be the proof
that I've lived.
Loved
Flown
Fallen
Broken
Drowned

And emerged back again after it all

Look up at the sky and you'll see
that the wind blows through
moving everything.

Even in the days that you feel you might melt,
and dissolve under the weight of everything;

even then, look up to the sky and feel
the wind blowing through,

through clouds, mountains, worlds;
through you,
through me.

Nothing last forever and, eventually,
even the suffocating pressure will go away.

Just be patient and wait for it.

Don't let it drag you down.

Always remember:

Half understood conversations are only that,
half understood.

There's always another half,
the one we didn't hear

Don't make up in your head
something that you don't know for sure.

Bunnies taught me
the happiness of small things.

They taught me to enjoy myself
and to enjoy company as well.

They taught me to jump
when I'm happy,
and to hide by my own
when I don't feel good.

They taught me to respect my times
and those of other persons' as well.

To give space when needed
and to show affection when it was welcomed

They taught me to be
curious and cautious at the same time,
to explore anything new.

Bunnies taught me to be happy.

There's no need to be
roaring like a firework,

no need to be explosive,
spectacularly soaring to the sky
for a short-lived minute of glory;

It's perfectly fine to be a firefly,

absolutely OK to shine at ground level
hidden between grass and tree roots.

I'm devastated to see
you in this state;
The magnitude of your downfall.

I would like right now
to shout at you,
to call you many names
and worst, even.

And yet I'm telling myself not to,
because right now, one word,
I know.

And I don't want to.

But I don't know how to help
and you're my brother, maybe not of flesh but
who cares.

And still I say nothing,
and I know that you know
that I know, and that you know
that right now
only you can save yourself

A mask over your mouth
made of softest net,
a mask over which you pour
your dark bitter coffee;

And you grind and grind down,
all the chunky pieces
that would be hard to digest
'til nothing's left but golden dust.

And you complain, that you have
to pour your coffee through the filter;
and you complain oh, how much effort it is,
well

How hard would it be to realize that
everybody else does the same
with you, and for you?

That everybody grinds down their bitterest,
darkest coffee chunks
so you don't have
to taste those?

Ranting and complaining
about the things you despise,
about all you don't like
in your life;

And sighing and refusing
when the thought of change
crosses your mind.

I said this before and
will repeat for you:
"Everybody wants their life to change,
but no one wants to change the way they live"

How are you going to get to new things
if you don't try new roads?

And I know,
breaking patterns is a constant effort, but

You won't get different results if you
don't stay off the beaten path

I didn't lie when I said I loved you
I never lied
to you for thirteen years.

I did,
I have loved you, but,
I already explained to you;

I grew, you didn't.
It's not anyone's fault,
things just happen like that.

Some persons are the way and
not the destination.
Or so it's said.

My love for you was over,
and you kept strangling me.

Now every time you talk to me I feel
as if you came from behind
to put your hands on my shoulders

(pressure)

As if you put all your weight on my back

(hold me down)

As if you didn't let me advance

(Let me go)

It seems as if
you learned nothing,
you forgot that
every time
someone has tried to put
a collar on my neck,

I run away

Let me go

I want to grow

Stated my boundaries
said "no".

Said "step back,
"my space, my place",
"my body, my home"
"my mind, my refuge";

Said "don't"
you're not welcome so close.

And you feel outraged?

Well, if you feel outraged by me
setting boundaries of
what is
and what feels
correct,
then that means you didn't respect me
at all.

Because if you did it wouldn't be
so infuriating to you
you wouldn't feel insulted;

And I wouldn't have been in the need
to tell you off-limits

Allow yourself to grow
out of situations,
out of people,
out of behaviours
that don't suit you anymore.

Some persons might say
that you've changed but,
Why should you keep
wearing on an ill-fitted garment?

There's a river flowing through our heads
and we can't help but try to
catch the swimming fishes.

Sit there and just look at them
as they swim away,
each one with a label tag,

"useless" "worthless" "ridiculous" "not enough"
"unlovable" "disgraceful"

Don't try,
there's no point in catching them,
for what?

Fishes can't live out of water,
they would struggle and
make a fuss and
hit you in the face,
repeatedly.

It's ok to look at them from afar,
to acknowledge their existence but,
what would you gain by fishing them out?

Just allow them to swim away.

You cannot keep your eyes off
the negative side.
You acknowledge the positive there, yes,
you're a balance,
but still;

The negative side is heavier on your scale.

And I understand,
when you say some people only see
what good things you have and forget
about those you haven't.
Or about how much effort it took you;
Sweat, blood and tears,
as we often say.

But you yourself forget,
about where you've come from,
and where you've managed to get.

And a lot of people is
worried sick about you.

But you can't see because you can't
keep your eyes off the negative side.

Even if
I think you're selfish on most occasions,

even if
I think you're way too childish, throw way too much
temper tantrums,
rant and complain in excess.

Even if
I think you don't have
enough responsibility of your own life,
or that you're wasting away
smoking and watching youtube all day.

Even if
I see you throwing out of your life everyone,
and everything,
when they're inconvenient to you and
to your routine.

Even after all that still,
I'm proud of you.
Because you're keeping yourself alive.

I'm proud of you
because you're trying.

I'm proud because at least
you acknowledge your flaws.

I'm proud because I know one day
you'll realize that
it's the day you'll start walking,
that you don't need to wait for
"When I have this" or "when I'm like that",
that the work starts on day one.

I love you,
I'm not going to dump you.

I'm proud of you

WHEEL OF FORTUNE

Winter, spring, summer and autumn
starts all over again, one after the other
every year, the same yet different.

I feared that winter would
leave me frozen to the core,
that we would become still,
drifting away;
my numb fingers trying to reach you,
predisposed fears due to the past season.

But,
instead,
I fell, cosy and warm in your bed

Hermes dazzled me
with his words and tricks,
charlatan, god of thieves,
taught me many things,
but left me feeling trapped
on his childish, obtuse wings.

Ares' smile, the charmest one,
bright in the tan face of a warrior god,
passionate,
put me through sheets of fire,
only to find that I was so cold
I needed to set everything ablaze.

And along came Hefaestus,
seemingly cold, collected,
severe;
Instead hard working, rumble thunder,
forged on the womb of volcanos yet
delicate, like the trinkets of a silver necklace.

By your side I don't feel like
I have to sell my art to survive
or that
I need to create to impress you.

You give me energy, you give me strength.

By your side I'm not dreaming,
or pressuring myself to do something.

By your side I'm working because
I feel like I can achieve it

It stands out greatly,
and becomes so funny,
the time gap that exists between
the complete healing and
the person who did the hurting
realising that something changed.

It's not that I ignore you,
it's not that 'I don't talk to you anymore'
It's just that I walked away
and stopped being your shadow.

I'm not mad at you,
you're just not the centre of my universe.
XOXO.

All the flowers you keep gifting me
for no reason at all
I keep putting them on
shiny, pretty glass jars,
just in case that one day
you decide to stop giving them
or in case it falls away
and dies

I swear to the gods you could
hold me whole with just your hands;

lifting me up when I'm
succumbing
and
restraining me in place when I'm
drifting away.

And you hold me there
with your hands only,
bringing me close to your heart
and
I swear to the gods I could
stay forever
counting the stars in your chest.

Careful,
forever is a dangerous word.

One after another,
a myriad of connected kisses,
they're not enough.

A touch so soft that tickles me,
never enough.

I am a monster,
asking for love from the centre of myself
and you patiently feed me,
but it's not enough.
I never have enough.

And I tie down this monster,
and try to hold you lightly,
less this might break.

But I guess
you're strong enough,
capable enough,
to handle this monster that
screams for your love.

Maybe I don't love you
as I have loved,
maybe my heart has become
more stone with each blow,
or maybe this is a rational love
instead of a passionate one.

But I do love you and
my heart does melt
and I do have a passion for you.

Maybe it's who we are or
maybe I don't know at all

What I do know is
it's taken so far
for me to learn, to realize
that love doesn't equal suffering,
that love can exist within
reasonable levels
and not feel like a continuous up and down
from mania to depression.

It has taken *you*
to know that love doesn't have to hurt

People asked for love advice
so many times to me in the past,
perceiving me as strong,
independent,
not knowing I also loved too much.

And I've spoken logical words
on a topic completely irrational,
as the matters of the heart
are not the same as those of coexistence.

And this will turn out to be
probably the shittiest love poem ever
but if I've ever offered one good advice
on this subject it would be to
stay with the one who:

Will see you no less strong when you break down,
remains by your side while you recover
and considers you no less of a Queen for being human.

Stay with the one who will
compete against you on farting

Don't wait for anyone
to go sit in the grass with you
If it's what makes you happy.

It's ok

Tune out your brain,
turn down the worries,
plug out your connections to the world and
reconnect them with the birds, the plants.

Root yourself.

Why do I feel as if
I've known you before?

Warrior sorceress that I am
always looking
subconsciously
for the recollections of a soul,
forming a jigsaw, puzzle
to solve.

Bound to the door,
in search of the key.

Recruiting,
to make it whole.

I lay pictures in front of me,
turning depictions of future,
just out of habit
When I'm in doubt,
when I'm afraid.

Everything goes so well
and that's the worst of
questionings.
Waiting for the moment it all collapse,
and last time it took thirteen years, but
it came crumbling down anyway.

And I lay swords and wands in front of me,
and cups full of water instead of wine,
out of habit,
when I'm afraid
Of the price I'll have to pay for this happiness.

And golds and stars tell me
"don't be silly, nor afraid,
you live in the present,
enjoy it, however much it lasts.
You don't need us"

COMPRESSION

Biaxial stress, forcing atoms to expand in other directions, potens to movement, arché kineseas; life, in itself, preventing the stagnation that means Death.

Did what was correct
and no one followed.

Did the right thing and
it made zero impact.

Cared,
and no one else did.

And I was throwing a tantrum,
like the kid that stands on
unattended whims.

Waiting for a pat on the head.

Childish validation,
carried out uselessly to adulthood.

We did our part, our duty,
would be nice if someone followed,
but it's not indispensable.

I never said thank you
I think;

Spiraling down
into a black hole
the Sun burning my skin
so deeply I thought I would boil
in darkness and heat.

Taking blame
for a crime that was not mine,
for a reason illogical,
for someone that did (not) deserve;

Fool, and blinded,
deaf to the world,
Arunima the only thing in my ears;
Walking like a living dead.

"Why are you lying?"

Cold
water over me
poured unexpectedly,
waking me up from that fever dream.

Thank you.

On tattered threads
I'm keeping my parts together
barely walking
after making it this far on the road
just because someone
decided to
stick out their foot and
plant it down, pulling on
the loose thread
of a sewn-shut old wound.

And everybody is
offering me sweet mellow words of comfort
hoping that they help me
to pull in that string and make the seam close;
but I'm still thinking that
if doesn't matter what I do I
end up in the same closed door
probably I'm the one at fault.

And I don't know what to do,
who or how should I be,
because I just
don't know how
not to be me

Go ahead
and misprize my loyalty,

I'm not blind,
and I know
the things I do and
the ones I don't, but,

for each one
that I've screwed
I've fixed two

And I don't say it with acridity,
just please do
go ahead
and undervalue my worth.

I'm not begging for that
which is not my right,
I'm not forcing anyone to do any
extra effort.

I'm not asking for the moon,
I'm demanding what's rightfully mine.
What my efforts have gained me.

I'm asking for that which
would set me free,
as my freedom is
my highest priority, value, asset.

I'm only asking for one extra small step
So I can leave.

I WANT TO LEAVE
I DON'T WANT TO BE THERE ANYMORE

I demand
to be given what is mine.

Intensément petillant,
too intense, too sparkling,
so much not many can handle;

Bubbly and aggressive,
a rainbow of emotions,
that some would catalogue as "unstable"
not knowing what I have inside,
without knowing what I've gone through.

Through hell and heaven,
through purgatory to espy
my sins and fears.

Of course I'll look "unstable"
if I'm in the middle of an earthquake

Excuse me for growing..
Excuse me for being human.

You say you're "tired"
whenever
anyone comes and asks,
But "tired" doesn't even begin
to convey this feeling of exhaustion;

Exhaustion of not having time,
of not having energy,
or even sometimes of not having any interests
to dedicate that energy to.

We say we're "tired"
because we cannot explain how it feels
to be exhausted of waking up.

Thus seems to be my karma in this life
to learn
letting things go
when they don't go my way.

To avoid
closed doors on the road
and reroute to get to destination.

To live
without closure,
just with fading things that
turn to that greyish land
in-between.

To template my temper
and know when
I should stop pushing.

Justifying myself
making me innocent
to my eyes

Taking advantage of a system
for all the times I didn't,
allowing me to do
what I most feared.

A fight deep within,
that of the sick
who doesn't want to feel impeded
that feels guilty for resting
when it's needed and recommended.

Accommodation of the self
from all the times that thought
'this is not enough to leave'
from all the times that stood,
putting more pressure on top
of an already contracted body.

The terrors acquired
from becoming a tool,
a spinning wheel part of the machine,
the eternal struggle against oneself,

Am I faking it
or is it real?

I don't want to talk,
what's the point.

I've told over and over
my reasonable needs,
those I need to function
to stay in.

I've warned over and over
of what might happen
and no one took it seriously,
I don't know what to say
to be heard.

I can't fight anymore against
the incompetency,
the lack of interest,
of care.

So I'll retreat,
I can't keep hitting my head
on this wall
of silence and ignorance.

I'll retreat,
and I'll heal
and I'll fight
and I'll win

Or I'll burn it down.

Bow your head down,
don't say nothing out loud.

Take everything that might be put on your shoulders
and don't dare to complain or remind over
that you, and all of them, are human beings,
with needs and craves.

Swallow or choke
whatever they decided from that funnel
to pour
onto your throat.

Stand in the rain
artificially created for your spirit to
break. Down. Bow. Down. Bend. Down.

Flexible is your surname and the number your id,
flexible to the convenience of them, not yours.

So bend down, more and more
until you think you might break
under the weight,
and then
bow down even more
handling all the rain with no hope,
no spark or light
in your soul.

Well,
not anymore.

I'll bend what I can,
what my abilities allow me to.

I'll stand in that shower of shit,
I'll even open my mouth
for you;
but don't think I'll do so without a soul,
don't dare to think that you can crush my hope,
I've been through worse
and my head, myself, I am my worst
enemy, after all.

Don't wish, don't hope
that I'll forget my humanity
that I'll not remind you of yours,
I was born to make others uncomfortable
after all.

And don't dream that I'll be standing there
under any kind of mistreatment you decide to
submit us to
and will not look you in the eye
and say it is bullshit
all while I do as you told
efficiently.

I'll stand, and I'll take, and receive
but not with my head and eyes down.

Now, it is my way, or no way at all.

Halted inhalation,
a deep breath without release,
clutched and held
inside a heart.

Counting the beats, waiting
to let it go,
so much air trapped
in these lungs that want to scream.

Taking oxygen in
like a free deep diver,
getting ready for immersion
liberation.

The throat itchy
from all this tension,
from all the deep breaths
taken,
from all the wants and will
to shout out
at last,
free.

CORE

Deep, in the centre of yourself,
a drumming song,
unknown yet familiar, that we rarely pay
attention to

I wished to become mute
so much when I was a kid.
Entitled, disrespectful, coming from a place of privilege;
but yes,
I wished, deeply,

To be deaf, so I wouldn't hear what anyone said,
so I didn't have to reply to them;

And to be mute,
so I didn't have to talk to anyone…

And thirty years may seem so long but
they're so few to understand

That what I wanted wasn't
to be deaf and mute.
What I needed was respect
of my boundaries.
What I was looking for was a space,
free and supportive,
where I could really speak up my mind.

I needed to find my voice,
rather than losing it.

Old me opened an eye and took a look
sweet golden liquor
oozing out of me
flowing up to my head
and making it float
popped up
like those years of black.

I don't like this.

Makes me trembles
from the earthquake installed on my chest and
I feel like shutting everyone
OUT.

Close the curtains and hide 'til
the shaking fades
But I'm afraid to stop.

Back then, I never moved and
it kind of feels as if
I've been climbing up a hill and if I
stop now
I'll roll back down.

It feels so strange to be me
Who am I?
Where am I?
Romantic and cynic,
eternal child, old and aged,
contradiction magnificent.

I don't know
Where it's me
Who is me

I am me but
Who am I?

And this body feels
strangling to my essence
and at times too big for me,
Excessively aware of the space it occupies.

Who am I?
What is it that is me?

Eternal,
unlimited and beyond.
Endless sea among stars.
Light and darkness.
All that and more.

Gagging noises out of my throat
something stuck, begging to come
out.

Started in the belly, a strange sensation,
of old things, fears,
rejections;
as a dark mass that had evaded
the light for too long, too much,
too deep and encysted.

This thing started to move,
slowly,
and finally I noticed it was there
like a parasite, a leech under my skin.

It was all so sudden, and strange,
because I didn't really do anything;
it was as if, after a massive cleaning,
only this dirt was left.

And so it started, a gagging noise in my throat
and a door in my dreams through which
throw out everything,
a lightbulb letting me see,
short-circuit in my brain and
all this darkness within
that started to come out
up and out, up and out

At moments I spat it,
others I just straight threw out,
extremely disgusting the times on which
I would have to bite a chunk
or swallow back down.

And it's still coming,
all this disgusting, stinky effluvium;
Coming from my self,
from others,
from reactions and
mostly from my childhood,

I see it now so clear.

I used to see the tree
imperfect and crooked,
too lively,
carried on the whims of
gusts of wind.
I saw its beauty and its strength;
But at the time when I observed
I barely felt human and,
by comparison,
it seemed too childish
too detached from reality.

If only I had known,
how deep its roots went
that its spawn
would end up resembling all that
she seemed to despise.

I see it on quirks,
on deliberated behaviours.

The spawn that prided herself
on its independence and autonomy,
finally understood what it means

to be flexible enough
to be carried away by the wind
and rooted deeply enough
to not let it blow herself completely away.

And all those things I
seemed to have so much disdain for
have turned out to be not so important,
not so terrible.

I'm still myself but,
the older I get,
the more I see I do
resemble my mother.

I am descendant
of a lineage of savage women,
of the women who lit up candles
and burned incense.

I come from the bloodline
of those who chose for themselves,
regardless of prejudices or social conventions,
of the women who
fought,
spoke too loudly,
spat in the faces of those
who tried to impose on them.

I come from my mother,
from my aunts,
grandmothers and great-grandmothers.

Strong women,
who loved greatly;
who dared, sometimes insanely.

Who got broken and
stood up yet again.

I am the lesson,
taught through their example.

And,
may they be present or not anymore,
in every step I achieve
I thank
to all the women in my family
for my education,
for who I am.

And doesn't matter
how much further I go
I know they guard my back

A contradiction magnificent
I like to call myself,
I am child and elder,
groundhog and eagle,
all at once and the same.

I say I do not know me,
or that I don't know
what is it that is me,
because I am all that at once
and the same.

I am an eagle,
yet I transform myself into a groundhog,
out of habit,
whenever I am out.
I have the spirit of a child
yet I wear a mask of adulthood,
out of habit,
whenever I am in the public.

Is there a real me,
and one fake?
Is the private me more real
because I feel freer to be
whenever I'm alone or
is it the public, the one people can see?
Maybe there isn't a 'real' one.

I have a coldness in my soul
that extends its fingers from my chest
to the world.
Uncalled.

I have a coldness deep within
that makes my hands sting
and my legs fall numb like steel.
It makes my eyes burn
and my lungs short of breath.

I have a coldness to heal
that says
no matter what I do is never enough.
Doesn't matter how much you try
you'll never get what's yours.

You'll always be that centaur,
hybrid of two worlds
that fits in none.

How much more do I have to give
so as to live in peace,
how much more do I have to put
as a sacrifice upon this shrine
for them to be satiated,
and not to rise this coldness within me.

Let me just be warm and cared

Pour your wishes unto a shooting star
but still you have to run after it
to watch them come true.

That's how magic works
that's how you actually do it.
By work, by focus,
every day.

The universe might have your back,
 and the opportunities will present themselves,
 but if you don't actively seize them,
 if you don't work, if you don't risk,
 it's as good as nothing.
The universe might have your back,
but ultimately
you must rely on yourself.

What's wrong with the word 'egocentric'?
What's wrong if I decide to be one?

Why is it wrong to decide to look
after oneself first?
Why is it wrong to state a fact and say
that we're our own centre?

Ultimately, we only have ourselves,
we can only rely on ourselves.
That will not prevent me from
loving and caring
sharing and enjoying.

It's so important to remember,
to keep your autonomy
for those who have a tendency to
give themselves away
completely.
And next thing you realize that you don't
want to do anything alone.

I'll share, I'll love
I'll build for both,
I'll give myself away, but
this time I'll remember
to keep a small piece for myself,
and to keep walking on my own two feet.

All along I knew,
all the meaning behind the nightmares
and the only solution.

All along the conclusion was there,
laid for me on a silver plate
that I just didn't want to take

I'll never outrun them,
I'll never be well hidden,
I can't pass unnoticed anywhere I go.

I'll be forever
stuck in-between realms
if I don't listen to myself,
if I try to please and not be seen,
renouncing all that it is me.

The only way
in which I could always win was
by flying.

I needed to learn to fly,
and goddamn if I did.

Everybody will stare,
they all will
and some even will try to catch me,
out of fear, or jealousy.

But the best days of my life were when
I didn't care and flew anyway.

That's what my rejection taught me:
to keep steady even after it.

So it seems time has come,
to fly again.

So fly.

Jump off that cliff and

FLY!

Home
where I can deflate,
where my bunnies are;
or

Home, where I spent my childhood,
where the impossible happens;
or

Home where I healed,
where the sea kisses the land
and the salty air makes everything shine.

Home where I get defensive,
home where I get territorial.

Home gone,
home where I either lose
my nerve or my freedom,
where I lack temperament and become apathy.

Home is comfortable,
and a comforted me is stagnant,

I will have to fight myself,
if I want to keep a home.

Home, will come soon,
when I learn to thrive.

How to accept
that what was done had a toll
that no one was to pay for.

How to take the blow
of the godly being fallible.

How to accept bearing it all
when no one was at fault,
when you have no one to blame
and dump your rage upon.

How to accept that,
after all,
we grow in the soil provided for us.

Take the blame out,
throw away resentment
and accept that
the soil you were planted in
might have not been a good fit;
that that ground affected
your roots for life,
even if you were bred
to the best of ability
with love and compassion.

So pick the earth from your stems
threshing all the parts,
removing the corrupted
putrid roots
and leaving only those
worth of nurture and care.

Break through the casket
encased shell of bones,
and bloom
in love and understanding
of it all.

The Goddess of the Universe
of light, all around you
in every colour and black hole.

The Goddess within,
the one who has my face,
myself.

The Goddess in every woman,
the one who has your face,
yourself.
The God inside every man.

The pure voice of the Universe,
unaltered.

You're going to make it,
resonate.

You're going to make it,
you are.

Tremble your feet,
for they want to walk;
tremble your hips
as they're willing to dance.

Trembles your stomach,
and your chest expands
wearing feathers of rainbow
that embrace all.

Rising and rising
in this whirlwind of light
that opens your insight,
filled like a cup,
overflowing on the purple,
ambrosia, a drug meant for angels.

Welcome back my child,
welcome back to you.

I'm sorry dear,
that you thought everything was your fault;
I'm sorry that you had to be a warrior,
I'm sorry that you had an ocean inside
dark and cold and unexplored.

I'm sorry I had to kill you to evolve.
I'm sorry that I still haven't figured out
who we are.

I'm sorry that I have opened your grave
and looked at your armour and weapons.
I'm sorry that I've thought about borrowing them
and burn everything down.

I'm sorry that I've tried to be you once more,
lost in the wrath and outrage,
in our fruitless territorial instincts.
I'm sorry for hiding in my bedroom,
and for losing all happiness from my flow.

But,
I'm glad to tell you that now I know
we can do better
that we are allowed to rest and be patient.

I'm glad to tell you that I've gone
where you never thought
and explored this ocean within,
and am still doing so.

I'm glad to tell you that now
we don't need to self-harm to feel
we are in control of our life.
I'm glad to tell you we can cry
and not feel useless,
that we can experience the full range of
our emotions without extremes,
that is not necessarily black or white
and that the peaceful in-between also
has its benefits.

I'm glad to tell you we're still looking
for freedom, but now we do
from a different position and perspective.
I'm glad to tell you we did things that
you'd never believe we did.

And I'm sorry that all of this is worthless,
and that you'd hate the person we've become
human.

But I'm glad to tell you that this person is
healthier, happier, stronger, resilient and hopeful.
This person doesn't want to die

I feel the sunshine
all over me,
I feel the light
tickling my skin,
making me laugh,
I feel free.

I might be walking
into another trap,
time might tell,
but for now I'm not afraid.

Ultimately, I will rely on myself,
on all these tasks I have ahead,
on this path that the light has shown,
and that might lead to a dream
(or not).

I see what I have achieved,
I see the pits, the fire,
and the cold.
Never forget.

But I also see now that
for each day walked
it's still a day more ahead
to keep walking on this path.

First and foremost, thank you for finishing this book; if you enjoyed it or have anything to say at all, I gladly welcome you to do so on your platform of preference, reviews are to authors like water is to plants.

MercuRea (Ana M. Valido) is a Spanish expat living in Netherlands; took to writing as a means to cope with anxiety disorder and explore the human emotions and psyche through alchemical and Jungian symbolism.

A lover of philosophy and mysticism in all of its variants, often considered as witch poetess due to the experiences lived, and always in research of knowledge of the true human Soul, the divine and nature.

If you want to keep up to date you can do so on Instagram and Facebook **@mercureaart**

Or collaborate with the small business to support indie self-published authors specialized in poetry at **@mercureaboekenhoek**

www.mercureaart.com

AUTHOR'S BIBLIOGRAPHY

Alchemy of the Soul: A collection of poetry. MercuRea. 2020. 120p. ISBN 9789090341774

Magic of Serene & Wild, an anthology by Dipika Singha. Rosewood publication. 2021. 352p.

The Silken hearts, an anthology by Zainul Arab O.H. Rosewood publication. 2021. 152p.

Inked from Heart, poetry compiled by Gurleen kaur and Shanjana Guruparan. Wordgenix publication. 2021. 144p. ISBN 9789354523106

Winner of my Heart, a compilation by Simarpreet Kaur. Spotwrite publications. 2021. 150p. ISBN 9788194918936

Benevolence, a poetry compilation by Divyanshu Rai and Simarpreet Kaur. Subharambh publication. 2021. 238p.

Your voice can make a change, a compilation by Simarpreet Kaur. Publishing experts. 2021.

**Corpus visita interiora
anima terrae**

**Anima rectificando
spiritus invenies**

**Spiritus occultum
lapidem corpus**